Spring Boot and Single-Page Applications

Securing Your API with a Single-Page
Application Frontend
second edition

Jens Boje

Spring Boot and Single-Page Applications
second edition
Jens Boje

ISBN-13: 9781694463555

Rev. 2.0

Published in 2019 by Jens Boje

Jens Boje
Pfungststr. 3
60314 Frankfurt
Germany

On the web: http://codeboje.de
Please send errors to book@codeboje.de

Publisher: Jens Boje

Table of Contents

README

Learning to build applications and especially APIs with Spring and Spring Boot is exciting. At the same time, it is freighting when you stay at the bottom of Mt. Spring.

Spring Boot makes it much easier than it was with Spring alone in the past. However, it also hides much of the complexity involved in its magic, which brings in new complexity and might leave you confused sometimes.

Be assured that this is totally normal and everyone went through this phase. When you hike up, it gets easier as you will gain a solid understanding and control of the complexity involved and you can build frictionless applications with it.

I know I felt this way when I first started out with Spring, and there was no Spring Boot at that time. But, that's temporary, and it gets much better over time. When I walked up Mt. Spring a bit, it already got easier. And it wasn't just me, I noticed the same with friends and co-workers.

In the book, I reduce the complexity and focus on small, manageable parts, so you get productive quickly. It is the same approach I use successfully in my workshops or when helping co-workers in-person. Unlike in-person interaction, I'm not with you to see you when you progress through the book. Therefore, I can't notice when you have a question so I can rephrase and explain it differently. Nonetheless, you are not alone, you can ask me, and I will help you get unstuck. Promise— just email me.

Introduction

This book's approach differs from that of other programming books that you may have encountered. That's because I believe that the best way to learn a new framework or language is to build applications using it.

We will build upon our sample microservice we created in the book "Spring Boot - How to get started and build a Microservice" and turn our attention to the different ways of integrating it with a single-page application (SPA). The main focus will be on security aspects. We will not cover the initial creation of the microservice here but concentrate on the communication side with a SPA.

The sample SPA is written in Angular 4 (and Typescript) and kept simple on purpose. It consists of a login screen for the admin, a paginated list of all stored comments, and an action to delete a single comment. I do cover it briefly, however, the focal point is on the Spring Boot side.

What we will build in this book

- Create a login in the SPA to connect with a stateless microservice using basic authentication and CORS.

- Use the same login but use JSON Web Tokens (JWT) instead of basic auth.

- Make our microservice stateful only for the authentication, use a form based login, and put an eye on CSRF.

- Combine the SPA and microservice in a single deployment application.

We are using Spring Security in the microservice.

The full source code for this book's sample applications is available on GitHub: Link (https://github.com/azarai/spring-boot-book-ui)

The code is split in a backend containing our Spring Boot microservice and a frontend with all the Angular 4 code. Each integration variant resides in its own branch.

I'll explain the most relevant code in the book with code samples. However, I do skip the code for certain simple helper classes but you can always find them in the source code.

What You Will Need

- Java 8+

- Maven (3.2+)

- Node JS

- Angular CLI

- Text editor or IDE of your choice. I use Spring Tools Suite and Visual Code Studio, but both are not required to follow along.

Installing and setting them up is not in the scope of this book.

Our Microservice

In the book "Spring Boot - How to get started and build a Microservice" we build a microservice for managing comments. The comments could be attached to pages, products, etc. We left this open and used a string identifier for the reference. In the end, we secured our API with basic authentication. It is a simple CRUD microservice, and for this book, we will add a new endpoint and solely work with the new one. To get you started, check out the essential service at the project repository (https://github.com/azarai/spring-boot-book-ui-2edition). The master branch contains the code we will build upon now.

Now we are going to extend the microservice with a new API endpoint for a simple admin interface we are going to implement in the next chapter.

The admin interface gets its own endpoint in our API for listing all comments. As we use it internally, we will return directly to our *Comment*, and as the response can get quite larger, we also add pagination to it.

So, let's start.

In the *CommentRepository*, we need a new method for retrieving a list of comments:

```
Page<Comment> findAll(Pageable pageable);
```

Pageable is part of Spring Data and indicates pagination information like sorting, current page, items per page, etc. It can be used in the method signatures and is automatically handled by Spring Data. You can combine it with custom query parameters, but you must put the special field at the end of the parameters.

When using pagination, Spring Data will return a Page with our model instead of a list. *Page* includes information about the total number of pages and items of our query, the current page with size, and values. With those, we can build a pagination later in the UI, and with *Pageable*, we can then specify which page and comments we want to retrieve.

Now let's add a simple method to the *CommentServiceImpl* and *CommentService* interface to make it available to the *Controller* class.

```
public Page<Comment> list(Pageable pageable) {
    return repository.findAll(pageable);
}
```

If your service classes only forward to the repositories and do not contain any additional logic, you can skip those and use the repositories directly in the controllers.

Spring also offers support of pagination in regular Web MVC Controller if we enable it with the *@EnableSpringDataWebSupport* annotation in our Spring configuration, ideally on the main application class. If you use the code from the repository, it is already added.

Now, we can use a *Pageable* object as a method parameter in any Spring MVC exposed methods. Spring will automatically transform the query parameters page and size and pass them down to us in the *Pageable* object.

With the *@PageableDefault* annotation on the method parameter, we can set defaults if query parameters might be missing. Also, we use it and set a default ordering by *creationDate* and show the recently created comments first.

Let's see that in action and we add the new endpoint */comments* to our *ReadController*.

```
@RequestMapping(value = "/comments")
public Page<Comment> listComments(
    @PageableDefault(sort={"creationDate"}, direction=
Direction.DESC)
    Pageable pageable
```

```
) throws IOException {
    LOGGER.info("list comments");

    Page<Comment> r = service.list(pageable);

    LOGGER.info("list comments - done");
    return r;
}
```

Now build the microservice and start it. Use Postman with our request collection (backend/SpringBootBook.postman_collection) or your favorite tool and create a few dozen comments via the */create* endpoint.

/comments will respond now with a list of max 5 comments and the pagination information. In the next chapter, we are going to explore the admin interface built with Angular 4.

Recap

Before we continue, let's review what we have covered and check your understanding with a short quiz.

- What is the Pageable interface used for in Spring Data?

- What is the Page interface used for in Spring Data?

- What does the @RequestParam annotation do?

Our Single-Page Application using Angular 4

The single-page application for this book is written in Angular 4 using the Angular CLI. Angular CLI (https://cli.angular.io/) is a command line interface for creating and working with Angular projects.

I build a simple admin interface to our freshly created */comments* endpoint. The admin supports only the Retrieve and Delete part of CRUD as they are enough to learn the concepts involved.

Let's start with a brief introduction into the SPA.

Getting Started

Clone the project from GitHub (https://github.com/azarai/spring-boot-book-ui). The SPA is in the *frontend* folder, and the relevant code we are covering is in *src/app*.

After cloning the repository, we need to install all dependencies of our application.

Open a terminal, move to the *frontend* folder, and run:

```
npm install
```

This will install the required modules in a subfolder named *node_modules*.

Angular offers a development server so that we can run it locally without external dependencies and test it in the browser.

You start it with:

```
ng serve
```

It starts the development server on port 4200, and you can access it with localhost:4200 in your browser. You should see the welcome screen of the application.

Project Structure

Base Application

The main entry of the application are the *app.component* files.

app.component.ts

Code of the component.

app.component.html

HTML aka Template of the component. It provides the main HTML of the page using Bootstrap and provides a point to plug in other components using the *router-outlet*.

app.module.ts

Defines which module are application uses.

app.routing.ts

Contains all routes aka URL's, aka pages available in our app.

home.component.ts

Simple welcome message with a link to comment list. It is the default route and not protected.

Commentlist

commentlist.component.ts

The component handling the listview of the comments including pagination. It uses the Angular ngx-bootstrap module for pagination. A click on a delete button triggers the confirmation dialog for the selected comment. On confirmation, it retrieves a callback by the confirmation dialog and triggers the deletion on the backend.

commentlist.component.html

Simple bootstrap 4 table with an action row containing the delete button per row and the pagination at the bottom.

comment.service.ts

Provides access to our API as an Angular service. It also sends the authentication credentials to our API with each request.

Confirm Dialog

confirmdialog.component.ts

A simple implementation of a confirmation dialog using Bootstrap 4 modals. Retrieves the selected comment as the input, displays the name of it in the confirmation dialog, and if the user confirms deletion with the delete button, it triggers a callback.

confirmdialog.component.html

HTML of the component using bootstrap 4 modal

Login

login.component.ts

The login screen for the application. Uses the *authentication.service* to log in the user.

login.component.html

Simple form with username, password, and a button using Bootstrap 4 forms.

Security

The login state of a user is held in localStorage under the key *currentUser*.

_guards/auth.guard.ts

Implements the *CanActivate* functionality of Angular and is responsible for checking if the user can activate a method, component or route.

authentication.service.ts

Provides login and logout methods for our UI, which will call the backend methods on our microservice.

Overview

The entry point of an Angular application is the *app.component*. In ours, we define the general HTML using Bootstrap 4 and provide a point where the other "pages" can plug in (*router-outlet*). The routes are set in *app.routing* and the sample application has one for the home page, one for the login form and one for the comment list.

The comment list is protected by an Angular Guard using *canActivate* in the routing declaration and specifying the guard in use.

When you first open the SPA in the browser, it starts the main application and routes you to the *home.component*. This one displays a simple message and a link to the comments list.

On clicking the link to the comments list, Angular will try to route us to the *commentlist.component*, detects that it is protected by an auth guard, and calls this one instead. Our *auth.guard* will check in localStorage if it contains the key "currentUser" for our application. If it is not available, as in the first use, *auth.guard* will redirect us to the login form.

In the login form, we enter the username and password (admin/ mypassword defined in *application.properties* in the microservice). The form calls our *authentication.service* for actually logging us in. On success, the current user with its token/credentials is stored in the localStorage and the user is redirected to its original page request, the comment list.

commentlist.component will load a table with all comments our microservice returns. It uses the */comments* endpoint we created in the previous chapter and supports pagination using the ngx-bootstrap Angular module.

For each comment, a delete button is displayed and backed by a confirmation dialog. On confirm, it will send a *DELETE* request for this comment to our API.

Take a few minutes to navigate through the frontend code. However, for the rest of the book, we will code only in *comment.service* and *authentication.service*.

Ready?

Then let's continue with an overview of the ways of integration in the next chapter.

Four Ways of Integration

In this chapter, we are going to discuss four popular ways to integrate your Spring Boot application with a single-page application. It works for any kind of application which exposes an API, whether for internal use and solely for your UI, or if the API is public.

In any case, you must know which user is calling your API, provide a way to login and logout the user, and prevent malicious side requests known as Cross-Site-Request-Forgery (CSRF).

On word in advance: When we talk about a state in this context, we are talking about authentication only, i.e. a stateful authentication is the classic session cookie. The microservice itself is stateless; it can do its job without having a state for domain objects.

The commonly used integrations are:

1. Stateless Microservice with Basic Authentication and support of CORS

2. Stateless Microservice with JWT as a token based authentication and support of CORS

3. Stateful Microservice using a form based login and support of CORS and CSRF

4. Stateful Microservice with the SPA integrated as a single deployable

The first three variants deploy the API and SPA as individual applications on different domains. The SPA is often accessible under app.example.com and the API under api.example.com. While this is not a problem when connection desktop or mobile clients, it involves a security concept in browsers called Cross-Origin Resource Sharing (CORS). In short, a resource can define which other domains can use it and how. And app.example.com and api.example.com are two different domains for the browser. We'll discuss more in the CORS section.

The SPA provides a login form and must log in into the API. It also keeps track of the authentication state.

The last variant is the standard approach of deploying the application on the same domain and in the same application. Here we can let the server side do the login and log out and use a default session mechanism for authentication.

All variants have pros and cons. We are going to implement all of these and discuss the pros and cons in the following chapters.

Cross Site Scripting (XSS)

Before we dive into the integration part, let's turn our attention to a topic which is extremely related.

XSS is an attack where a bad guy smuggles code into our application via data entry and the code gets executed when a user visits a page with the manipulated content.

This attack needs two prerequisites to work. First, a user must be able to submit code. This can either be in any field of user generated content or even when importing data from third parties.

Second, our application only displays its content plain so a browser would interpret it as valid HTML with Javascript and execute it.

To eliminate this risk, we must check all user inputs and remove HTML and unwanted characters or at least escape them in a form that they are no long valid HTML. In the case of our comment store, we could add this code in the service layer before we save, or even better process the comment. Or add it directly in the *Controller*.

The Prevention Cheat Sheet (https://www.owasp.org/index.php/XSS_%28Cross_Site_Scripting%29_Prevention_Cheat_Sheet) collects some realistic rules for tackling that problem.

The other thing we should do is not to display user entered content as it is, but also escape all HTML before display. Now it will not be interpreted by the browser.

Usually, the major SPA frameworks do the "escaping on display" by default.

Make sure to remove/escape unwanted characters when inserting data and also escape them on display.

Code

Each variant is in its own branch in the book project on GitHub (https://github.com/azarai/spring-boot-book-ui).

Stateless Microservice with Basic Auth and CORS

This is the first variant we are implementing. You can find the source code in the *stateless_basic_auth_cors* branch.

Overview

In a browser-based Single-page application and an API backend, we have three components involved.

* the SPA

* the API

* and the Browser as it adds some security features

Figure 1 shows how the components interact with each other in our first step.

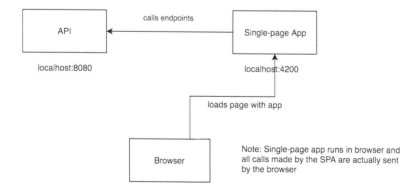

Figure 1: API and SPA with basic auth

The API at this stage is stateless, i.e. the server-side does not keep track of any logged in user states. This also means, that each request must contain login credentials for authentication.

The SPA and API run on their own individual port. We point the Browser to the host of the SPA, and it loads and executes it. The Javascript is now running in the Browser, and thus its security and sandboxing concepts are in place. The SPA running in the Browser now makes the calls to our API.

The two different ports, even on the same host, are already treated by the Browser as two different domains. It is the same as the SPA was loaded on example.com and the API resides on api.example.com.

The restriction the Browser enforces is called Cross-Origin Resource Sharing, and we will cover it later in the chapter.

In the first version, the calls to the API are protected by basic auth. This means that the SPA has to send the users credentials in a Base64 encoded format with every single request to the API.

The SPA asks the user once for their username and password and then stores the credentials in the browser local storage, which is only accessible by code loaded from the same domain as our app (Figure 1b).

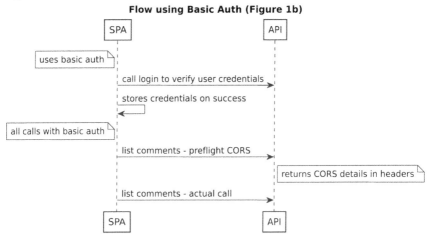

Flow using Basic Auth (Figure 1b)

16

Implementation

When we added the Spring Security Starter in the previous book, it automatically set up a basic auth and our API was protected. However, we need more control now and will override the security configuration.

For that, we add the new class *WebSecurityConfig* along the *CommentStoreApp* and annotate it with *@Configuration* so it will get picked up during start up as a configuration and we enable web security with *@EnableWebSecurity*.

In the case of securing a Spring MVC application with Spring Security, our configuration extends *WebSecurityConfigurerAdapter* and overrides certain methods.

```
@Configuration
@EnableWebSecurity
public class WebSecurityConfig extends
        WebSecurityConfigurerAdapter {

}
```

For configuring web security, we must override the *configure* method and set it up manually.

```
@Override
protected void configure(HttpSecurity http) throws
Exception {
    http.csrf().disable()
    .sessionManagement()
    .sessionCreationPolicy(SessionCreationPolicy.STATELESS)
    .and()
    .authorizeRequests()
        .anyRequest()
            .authenticated()
             .and()
                    .httpBasic();
}
```

First, we disable CSRF protection in this variant as we do not need it. We'll see why later on.

Next, we configure the session management of the servlet container and set it to stateless. The JSESSIONID Cookie is gone.

```
.sessionManagement()
.sessionCreationPolicy(SessionCreationPolicy.STATELESS)
```

And then we declare basic auth for all endpoints.

```
.authorizeRequests()
  .anyRequest()
    .authenticated().and().httpBasic();
```

However, basic auth needs some users. For this example, we are going to provide an in-memory store (*inMemoryAuthentication*) with a simple admin user (*withUser*).

We also must declare a *PasswordEncoder* for encoding password as nobody wants to store passwords in plain text. Add one with:

```
@Bean
public PasswordEncoder passwordEncoder() {
    return new BCryptPasswordEncoder();
}
```

Now, create the *configureGlobal* method and annotate it with *Autowired*:

```
@Autowired
public void configureGlobal(
    AuthenticationManagerBuilder auth

) throws Exception {
    auth.inMemoryAuthentication()
    .withUser("admin")
    .password(passwordEncoder().encode("mypassword"))
    .roles("ADMIN");
}
```

It is picked up by Spring Security now as a global configuration of the *AuthenticationManagerBuilder* in case we have multiple security configurations active.

We can directly use the *passwordEncoder()* to get the encoder and encode our password as it is our responsibility when creating users.

When you start the Spring Boot application now, you can use basic auth as before with curl or Postman. The next step is to prepare the SPA.

The login in the SPA is handled in the *authentication.service*. The *login* method performs a request to our API (*/authenticate*) using the credentials from the form and if it succeeds, these are valid.

It creates the *authorization* header for basic auth and calls */authenticate*. If the response is an HTTP status 200, the credentials are valid. We then store the value of the *authorization* header with the username in the localStorage.

Theoretically, we could use any simple endpoint in our API for validating basic auth. However, it's good practice to have a specific one for this task.

```
login(username: string, password: string) {
  let headers: Headers = new Headers();
  let authHeaderValue = "Basic " +
                        btoa(username + ":" + password);

  headers.append("Authorization", authHeaderValue);
  let options = new RequestOptions({ headers: headers });

  return this.http.get(this.server + "/authenticate",
    options).map(
    (response: Response) => {
      if( response.status === 200) {
          localStorage.setItem('currentUser',
            JSON.stringify(
                { user: username,
                  token: authHeaderValue
                }
            )
        );
    }
  });
```

For this authentication request to work, we create a new *LoginController* in the microservice.

```
@Controller
public class LoginController {

    @RequestMapping("authenticate")
    @ResponseStatus(code=HttpStatus.OK)
    public void authenticate() {

    }
}
```

The endpoint has no custom logic. The SPA provides the credentials as basic auth in the *authorization* header, and Spring Security does check them in the security filter chain. Only when valid is our method invoked. Using *@ResponseStatus* it returns only an HTTP status 200.

In addition, we also must add the *Authorization* header on each subsequent request. *comment.service* does handle it for our UI. We can pass additional options to the Angular HTTP service and set the header to the value we receive from localStorage.

```
public getComments (page:number) {
  return this.http.get(
      this.server + "/comments?page=" + page,
      this.getAuthHeader()).map(this.extractData
  );
}

private getAuthHeader() {
  let user = JSON.parse(
                    localStorage.getItem('currentUser')
  );

  let headers: Headers = new Headers();
  headers.append("Authorization", user.token);
  let options = new RequestOptions({ headers: headers });
  return options;
}
```

Start the microservice and the development server of the frontend and point your browser to *localhost:4200*. When you try to log in now, you will notice that it still fails. In the dev console in Chrome or Firefox, you'll see an error message telling you that access to this resource is denied. That's CORS.

localhost:4200 and *localhost:8080* are two different domains for the browser and our request is, therefore, cross domain. The browser will prevent it as we didn't explicitly allow this usage in our API.

Cross-origin resource sharing (CORS)

The browser checks for CORS in a two-step process. First, it analyzes the request. If it is GET or HEAD and we use no custom headers, it executes the request as is. For any other request, it does a pre-flight. For the pre-flight, it sends an OPTION request to the same endpoint with a *Origin* header set to the domain the script was executed from and checks some response headers if the request is allowed.

The main headers are

- Access-Control-Allow-Origin contains a list of allowed domains or * for all.

- Access-Control-Allow-Methods contains a list of allowed HTTP methods.

If the pre-flight is successful, it will actually call the resource as requested. If the pre-flight fails, it denies access.

Let's change that.

First, we activate support of CORS in our security config in *WebSecurityConfig*. Add the following after *.csrf().disable()*

```
.cors()
```

It will support preflight for our endpoints and also for auto-configured security endpoints when in use, i.e. form based login URL's.

Next, we must configure CORS in Spring MVC. We can configure it with the *@CrossOrigin* annotation for each *Controller*, or endpoint, or with a global configuration.

We will use the global configuration. Create the new class *WebConfig* along with the other configuration classes and extend from *WebMvcConfigurerAdapter* so we can override the CORS settings.

```
@Configuration
public class WebConfig extends WebMvcConfigurerAdapter {

    @Override
    public void addCorsMappings(CorsRegistry registry) {
        registry.addMapping("/**")
            .allowedOrigins("http://localhost:4200")
            .allowedMethods("GET", "DELETE")
            .allowedHeaders("*")
            .allowCredentials(true)
            .maxAge(3600);
    }
}
```

Let's take a look at the individual settings.

• addMapping defines the endpoints for this CORS configuration.

• allowedOrigins configures the Access-Control-Allow-Origin header.

• allowedMethods configures the Access-Control-Allow-Methods header.

• allowedHeaders specifies which headers are allowed in the requests.

• allowCredentials allows the sending of credentials, i.e. session cookies in cross-origin requests.

• maxAge defines in seconds how long the browser can cache this information.

The actual values highly depend on your scenario. If you provide a public API, you are probably going to allow all origins and methods used in your API.

If it is only used by your applications or a small group of customers, I'd limit the origins to those systems. I'd even do so when the applications are only used internally.

However, when you restart the comment store now and try to log in, it will work. You'll see a list of comments and can delete single ones.

Conclusion

Now that we have covered the technical side, let's discuss the solution.

Basic auth is a simple authentication mechanism and widely supported. It also has a low overhead; both in terms of the size of the string and processing time for de- and encoding.

The username and password are only entered once per user session on the client, and the encoded auth string is stored in localStorage. Localstorage, by design, can only be accessed by scripts loaded from the same domain.

The actual authorization on the back end is done with a header.

When the bad guy tries to lure our user into a trap, he'd need to set a custom header on each forged request. For that, he needs either the username and password or the encoded auth string. The first two are only typed in once, and the other is stored in localStorage.

Modern browsers support CORS and assuming the implementations work, a CSRF attack won't work.

However, if somehow the browser had a bug and the bad guy can access the auth token, he still needs to pass the cross-origin limits. If we limit it to our application, he'd still not pass.

The bad guy could attack the application with the help of XSS. If he manages to run code on our site, he can extract the credentials from localStorage and post them to his own back end. He now has the username and password and could log in. And as users tend to use the same password for multiple sites, he might gain access to more.

I think this possibility is the only real drawback when using basic auth in a consumer facing.

One other con people often claim is that you need to load the user on each request in the back end to validate the credentials and load the user's rights. However, in most cases, it is a simple database call with less overhead, in latency and payload size, and can be ignored.

It can cause trouble if your user authentication or the loading of user details either makes many calls to a database or is even calling other web services. This can definitely slow down your authentication.
However, instead of switching to another auth schema, I'd advise you to find the real cause and fix it.

We did have exactly the "performance problems" for logins in a recent project of mine. The cause of this was spaghetti code in the user management component. It loaded the user several times and due to some JPA relations, it loaded users who weren't even related to the request even more.

Keep the user authentication and authorization part slick.

Recap

Before we continue, let's review what we have covered and check your understanding with a short quiz.

- How do we validate the user credentials?

- Do we pass a session or token back from the back end to the SPA?

- Which are the main headers for CORS?

- How do you configure CORS globally in Spring Boot?

- Can a potential attack steal the credentials from localStorage?

Stateless Microservice with JWT Auth and CORS

In this alternative, we are moving from basic auth to using JSON Web Tokens. You can find the source code in the *stateless_jwt_cors* branch.

Overview

We have the same components and structure as in the previous version (Figure 2).

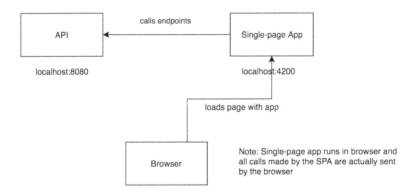

Figure 2: API and SPA with JWT auth

The major difference is now that we authenticate with a token instead of sending the Base64-encoded credentials along. Principally, it fulfills the same purpose. A token is just another form of credentials. And thus shall be handled like all other credentials; with care.

Although, we will have one request at login time, which does not use a token because we don't have one yet. This first login is still made using basic auth, and as a result, we retrieve a token for all subsequent requests (Figure 2b).

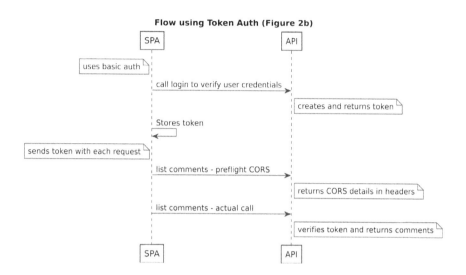

As API and SPA are still on different hosts, CORS does also apply.

The SPA will now store the token in the Browser's local storage instead of the previous user credentials.

Introduction to Token and JWT

When people are moving away from basic auth, a natural path is to switch to some kind of token authorization. Instead of the basic auth string, we now use an arbitrary token with no data encoded or other meaning. It is a simple string as the value in a JSESSIONID cookie. Instead of a cookie, the token is received by the client as the result of a successful authentication request, stored in localStorage on the client and sent with each subsequent request in the *authorization* header.

The back end has to keep track of each token and which user it represents and needs to load the mapping and the user's rights on each request from some storage.

JSON Web Tokens are a method which tries to solve the latter problem and transport rights securely between applications. The rights or other custom data are stored encoded in the token itself. So the token could include the username and the rights of the user. A party, i.e. our back end, could just decode the token and use the username and rights included. To prevent anyone from tampering with the data, the token is digitally signed.

JWT's are split into three parts separated by dots.

- Header: contains token type (JWT) and the algorithm used for the signature

- Payload: custom data we can transport, like a username and/or rights aka claims

- Signature: the signature build with the specified algorithm using header and payload.

For more insight on the implementation details, check out Introduction to JSON Web Tokens (https://jwt.io/introduction/).

Implementation

Unfortunately, JWT does not work out of the box with Spring Security and we have to implement it ourselves which requires a few extra steps.

We are going to use the JWT implementation provided by Stormpath. Add the following dependency to your pom.

```
<dependency>
    <groupId>io.jsonwebtoken</groupId>
    <artifactId>jjwt</artifactId>
    <version>0.7.0</version>
```

```
</dependency>
```

Login and JWT Generation

We are going to request the */authenticate* endpoint and still use basic auth for the login. However, we will now return a JWT and use it in the SPA for each request.

In the *LoginController*, we use the current logged in user and create a token for him. The currently logged in user can be passed as a method parameter and is automatically added by Spring MVC. *Authentication* represents details of an authentication request and is a core part of Spring Security. From it, we obtain our custom user which is stored as the principal in Spring Security. By default, Spring Security will use its own *User* class, and for the sample, we will stick with it.

Next, we call *JWTGenerator*, which we will implement shortly, retrieve the token, and return it as a response. *@ResponseBody* makes sure we return our token as the response body.

```
@RequestMapping("authenticate")
@ResponseStatus(code=HttpStatus.OK)
@ResponseBody
public String authenticate(Authentication authentication) {
    final User user = (User) authentication
                        .getPrincipal();
    return jwtGen.create(user);
}
```

Create *JWTGenerator* in *de.codeboje.springbootbook.commentstore.security.jwt*

```
@Component
public class JWTGenerator {

    @Autowired
    private JwtSettings settings;

}
```

JwtSettings is a custom class using Spring Boots *@ConfigurationProperties* mapping mechanism. The values are set in *application.properties* and mapped and type-checked by Spring Boot during startup.

- tokenIssuer identifies us, either as a name or using our base URL

- tokenSigningKey the key used for signing

- tokenExpirationTime an expiration time, how long the token is valid

Next, we create the *create* method and start to generate the token.

```
public String create(User user) {
    Claims claims = Jwts.claims()
            .setSubject(user.getUsername());

    claims.put("scopes",
        user.getAuthorities()
            .stream()
            .map(s -> s.toString())
            .collect(Collectors.toList()));

    Instant currentTime = Instant.now();


    String token = Jwts.builder()
      .setClaims(claims)
      .setIssuer(settings.getTokenIssuer())
      .setIssuedAt(Date.from(currentTime))
      .setExpiration(
          Date.from(currentTime.plus(
              settings.getTokenExpirationTime(),
              ChronoUnit.MINUTES))
      )
      .signWith(SignatureAlgorithm.HS512,
          settings.getTokenSigningKey()
      )
    .compact();

    return token;
}
```

Claims are basically the payload we are transporting. The *Subject* is one of the standards and defines for whom the token is; in our case, we assign the username.

Then we add a custom claim named *scopes* and set it to all authorities of the user. *Authorities* contain the rights and roles a user has and is part of Spring Security.

Afterward, we use the *Jwts* module and its *JwtBuilder* to create the token.

Now, we can successfully auto wire it in *LoginController*

```
@Autowired
private JWTGenerator jwtGen;
```

And upon the next authentication request, we should receive a valid token.

On the client side, we retrieve now the token on a successful authentication and store it as before in localStorage.

In *authentication.service* we get the token by calling *response.text()* and assign it accordingly. Your code should look like:

```
localStorage.setItem('currentUser',
    JSON.stringify(
        { user: username, token: response.text()}
));
```

In *comment.service* we change the *Authorization* header in *getAuthHeader* to *Bearer* and add the token like before.

```
headers.append("Authorization", "Bearer " + user.token);
```

When you start back and frontend now, you should be able to log in, and in the browsers network debugger, you see that all subsequent requests include the token in the *Authorization* header.

However, access is denied as Spring Security still doesn't know anything about the token.

Handling Authentication

For adding our custom JWT authentication, we need to plug into Spring Security on three points.

1. With a filter in the Spring Security Filter chain

2. With a Authentication implementation for our token based auth

3. With a provider class which can handle our Authentication implementation and authenticates the user

The job of a filter is to check if it is responsible for the incoming request, extracting the authentication information from the request and returning a *Authentication* instance.

The *Authentication* holds information and the state of an authentication request.

And the provider is used by the *AuthenticationManager* to handle the login for certain authentication requests.

Let's start with the filter and create *JwtAuthenticationProcessingFilter*.

```
public class JwtAuthenticationProcessingFilter
    extends AbstractAuthenticationProcessingFilter {

    private final AuthenticationFailureHandler
    failureHandler;

    private final JwtRequestExtractor tokenExtractor;

    @Autowired
    public JwtAuthenticationProcessingFilter(
        AuthenticationFailureHandler failureHandler,
        JwtRequestExtractor tokenExtractor,
        String path
    ) {
        super(path);
        this.failureHandler = failureHandler;
        this.tokenExtractor = tokenExtractor;
    }
 }
```

The *AuthenticationFailureHandler* is responsible for returning a response to the client in case of an authentication failure. *JwtRequestExtractor* is an implementation by us which extracts the token from the header. And the *path* parameter in the constructor defines for which path our filter should run.

For simplicity, we extend *AbstractAuthenticationProcessingFilter* which supports a standard process in the authentication request. We override some behavior.

The method *requiresAuthentication* determine if a request requires authentication for the filter.

```
@Override
protected boolean requiresAuthentication(
    HttpServletRequest request,
    HttpServletResponse response
) {

    if (super.requiresAuthentication(request, response)) {

        if (HttpMethod.OPTIONS.name()
            .equalsIgnoreCase(request.getMethod())
        ) {
            return false;
        }

        Authentication existingAuth = SecurityContextHolder
                                    .getContext()
                                    .getAuthentication();

        if (existingAuth == null ||
            !existingAuth.isAuthenticated()
        ) {
            return true;
        }
    }

    return false;
}
```

We are ignoring all OPTIONS requests as it prevents CORS preflight and we also don't run if the user is already authenticated, i.e. after basic auth on the */authenticate* endpoint.

Next, we override the actual authentication attempt, and extract the token from the header using the *JwtRequestExtractor* and create an instance of our *Authentication* implementation.

```
@Override
public Authentication attemptAuthentication(
    HttpServletRequest request,
    HttpServletResponse response

) throws AuthenticationException,
        IOException,
        ServletException {

    return getAuthenticationManager()
        .authenticate(new JwtAuthenticationToken(
            tokenExtractor.extract(request)
                        )
    );
}
```

In addition, we override the default behavior of authentication success and failure with *successfulAuthentication* and *unsuccessfulAuthentication* and prevent the use of the rememberMe service, etc.

In the next step, we are implementing *JwtAuthenticationToken* and extend the base class *AbstractAuthenticationToken*. It is a simple data class containing our token, user, and an authentication state for Spring Security.

```
public class JwtAuthenticationToken extends
AbstractAuthenticationToken {

    private String token;
    private User user;

    public JwtAuthenticationToken(String unsafeToken) {
        super(null);
        this.token = unsafeToken;
        this.setAuthenticated(false);
    }

    public JwtAuthenticationToken(User user,
        Collection<? extends GrantedAuthority>
        authorities
```

```
    ) {
        super(authorities);
        this.eraseCredentials();
        this.user = user;
        super.setAuthenticated(true);
    }

}
```

The first constructor is used by our filter above and the second will be used by our provider in the next step. Furthermore, we override the getter for the credentials and principal and return our values. When credentials are erased in the workflow, we remove the token.

```
@Override
public Object getCredentials() {
    return token;
}

@Override
public Object getPrincipal() {
    return this.user;
}

@Override
public void eraseCredentials() {
    super.eraseCredentials();
    this.token = null;
}
```

Create the *JwtAuthenticationProvider* class and implement the *AuthenticationProvider* interface. This requires us to have *supports* and *authenticate* methods. The support method determines if our provider is responsible for a certain *Authentication* class and *authenticate* is doing the actual authentication.

The class also needs the *JwtSettings* injected for validating the token.

```
@Component
public class JwtAuthenticationProvider implements
AuthenticationProvider {

    private final JwtSettings jwtSettings;
```

```
    @Autowired
    public JwtAuthenticationProvider(
        JwtSettings jwtSettings
    ) {
        this.jwtSettings = jwtSettings;
    }

    @Override
    public boolean supports(Class<?> authentication) {
        return (JwtAuthenticationToken.class
                .isAssignableFrom(authentication)
        );
    }
}
```

In *authenticate* we get the *Authentication* as a parameter. We retrieve the
token via the *getCredentials* getter and validate the token in the
parseClaims method. If the validation fails, it will exit with an exception
and on success, we extract the username and rights from the token,
create a new *User* and authenticated *JwtAuthenticationToken* and return
it to Spring Security.

```
@Override
public Authentication authenticate(
        Authentication authentication
) throws AuthenticationException {

    String rawAccessToken = (String) authentication
                                 .getCredentials();


    Jws<Claims> jwsClaims = parseClaims(
                        jwtSettings.getTokenSigningKey(),
                        rawAccessToken
    );

    String subject = jwsClaims.getBody().getSubject();
    List<String> scopes = jwsClaims.getBody()
                        .get("scopes", List.class);

    List<GrantedAuthority> roles =
                    new ArrayList<GrantedAuthority>();

    for (String scope : scopes) {
        roles.add(new SimpleGrantedAuthority(scope));
    }
```

```
    final User user = new User(subject, „na", roles);

    return new JwtAuthenticationToken(user,
                             user.getAuthorities());
}
```

The *parseClaims* simply uses the *JwtParser* with our *signingKey* to extract the claims from the token. In the case of an error, we throw a *BadCredentialsException* with some details.

```
public Jws<Claims> parseClaims(
      String signingKey,
      String token
) {
   try {
      return Jwts.parser()
              .setSigningKey(signingKey)
              .parseClaimsJws(token);
   } catch (UnsupportedJwtException |
           MalformedJwtException |
           IllegalArgumentException |
           SignatureException ex
   ) {
      logger.error("Invalid JWT Token", ex);
      throw new BadCredentialsException
                     ("Invalid JWT token: ", ex);
   } catch (ExpiredJwtException expiredEx) {
      logger.info("JWT Token is expired", expiredEx);
      throw new BadCredentialsException
                     ("JWT Token expired", expiredEx);
   }
}
```

Now that we have done the heavy lifting, the only thing left is to configure Spring Security in our *WebSecurityConfig*.

First, inject our *JwtAuthenticationProvider*:

```
@Autowired
private JwtAuthenticationProvider
jwtAuthenticationProvider;
```

And then we must add the provider in the *configureGlobal* method:

```
auth.authenticationProvider(jwtAuthenticationProvider);
```

Now, we move our version of the *configure* method to a second *Configuration* class, which can either be a subclass or standalone. We do that because we need a setup *AuthenticationManager* for the next stage and can't do it in the same class.

Create *ApiSecurityConfig* and annotate it with *@Configuration* and *@Order*. The *@Order* annotation defines here a processing order of the configuration classes.

```
@Configuration
@Order(1)
public class ApiSecurityConfig extends
        WebSecurityConfigurerAdapter {

    @Autowired
    private RestAuthenticationEntryPoint
    restAuthenticationEntryPoint;


    @Autowired
    private AuthenticationFailureHandler failureHandler;

    @Autowired
    private AuthenticationManager authenticationManager;

    protected JwtAuthenticationProcessingFilter
    buildJwtTokenAuthenticationProcessingFilter()
    throws Exception {

        JwtAuthenticationProcessingFilter filter =
            new JwtAuthenticationProcessingFilter
                (failureHandler,
                 new JwtRequestExtractor(),
                 "/**"
            );

        filter.setAuthenticationManager(
                this.authenticationManager
        );

        return filter;
    }
}
```

RestAuthenticationEntryPoint is a simple handler that returns an HTTP 401 instead of the default redirect to a login page.

As the *AuthenticationFailureHandler*, our *JwtAwareAuthentication-FailureHandler*, which we have not covered as code here, is picked up and it also returns a 401 on authentication failures, i.e. the JWT is expired.

You can check both classes in the source code.

buildJwtTokenAuthenticationProcessingFilter instantiates our *JwtAuthenticationProcessingFilter*, assigns the used *AuthenticationManager*, and maps it to all paths.

Now, we configure our entry point with:

```
.exceptionHandling()
.authenticationEntryPoint(restAuthenticationEntryPoint)
```

right after disabling CSRF and after configuring basic auth, we set up the new *JwtAuthenticationProcessingFilter*.

```
.and()
    .addFilterAfter(
            buildJwtTokenAuthenticationProcessingFilter(),
            BasicAuthenticationFilter.class
    )
```

It will run after the *BasicAuthenticationFilter*, which is responsible for basic authentication so we can still use basic auth for the login.

Start both applications and you can login and view the comment list now.

Conclusion

This solution shares the same benefits with the previous one. We use the same CORS configuration as before with the basic auth example, and also store the token in localStorage on the client side.

The authentication is also sent in the *authorization* header.

So, in regards to attacks by the bad guys, we are on the same level as before.

There are however a few differences which add additional benefits but also constraints.

First, if an attacker somehow gets a hold of the token, he gains access to the API but he still does not get the password of the user and therefore other accounts of the same user are not in danger. In the browser, the attacker would still be limited by CORS and one would need to infiltrate your application via XSS.

If, however, he can get our token for outside attacks, he has full access to your API as the owner of the token. With the basic auth, you could change the password of the user and the bad guy loses access.

With the JWT, he still does have access to the API as long as the token is still valid. If you issued a timeless token, it's valid forever unless you implement some kind of blacklist (which you should, btw)

You can reduce the lifespan of a token to a few seconds or minutes but then you need to introduce some kind of token refreshing or it will get annoying for your users.

On the back end you can stop loading user data from a database when you store the essentials for the API in the token itself. However, a token can be easily decoded and the payload is not private. Besides that, the token grows in size the more claims you store in it. If you go with a minimum, you might actually gain some performance on the back end.

Also, in the previous version you were able to change the rights of a user on the fly. They'd be used on the very next request. With JWT your rights are stored in the token and you cannot simply remove one. You would need to issue a new token and render the old one invalid. Ideally, you would create a blacklist like mentioned before.

You can exchange some of the minor arbitrary data of your user between your API and SPA in the token and you might spare an extra endpoint. Just don't flood it and reduce the sensitive information to a bare minimum.

I think the advantages of the JWT pay off the most when used in communication between your microservices. You can spare the extra roundtrips to a user management and solely work on the claims in the JWT. Also, your services do not need dependency on your user management.

Recap

Before we continue, let's review what we have covered and check your understanding with a short quiz.

- Can you explain what a JSON Web Token is?

- What role is played by the filter we added?

- What is the job of the JwtAuthenticationProvider?

- Is the payload of a JWT secret?

Stateful Microservice with Form Auth, CSRF, and CORS

In this chapter, we are switching to a stateful authentication for our API. You can find the source code in the *session_cors_csrf* branch.

I started this example on the base of our first stateless variant with basic auth. You can start there and follow along or just use the source code from the branch above.

Overview

In this version, the SPA and API are still located on different hosts, but this time we make the API stateful and leverage Browser support a bit more. Figure 3 shows the overall components.

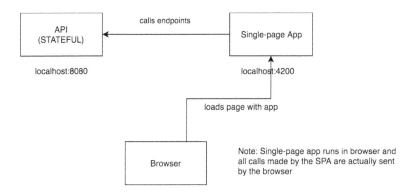

Figure 3: API and SPA with Form-based Auth and Stateful

The major difference to the previous versions is that we make the API now stateful. In this context, the authentication state is stateful, meaning the backend application keeps track of the user's authentication state. The other functionality of the API can still be stateless.

This is a classic version. The user logs in via a form, the server issues a session cookie and all subsequent requests are sent with the cookie, and thus the user is authenticated. It is a browser feature we are suing here. A Browser will always send domain cookies, aka cookie set on the same domain, along with each request to the domain (Figure 3b).

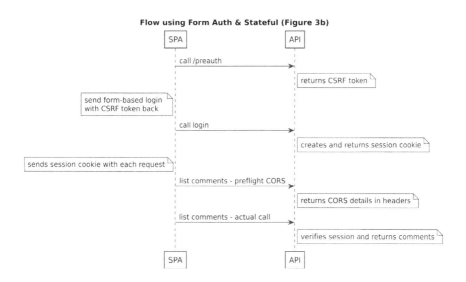

Flow using Form Auth & Stateful (Figure 3b)

This has some downsides and is/was a major attack scenario for malicious requests made by third parties called Cross-Site Request Forgery. Fortunately (CSRF), there are ways to protect against that, and we will implement the most common CSRF protection.

The form is shown in the SPA, and its server-side part is now handled in the API.

43

Implementation

In this example, we are going to use the form based login in Spring Security, adjust it a bit for working in a rest style pattern, keep CORS and basic auth as an optional authentication way, and protect our stateful authentication against CSRF attacks.

In stateful authentication, we can leverage existing mechanisms like the session cookie for authentication. So, the first thing we do is turn our API to stateful. For that remove the session management configuration in *WebSecurityConfig*, and Spring Security will auto configure stateful again.

```
.sessionManagement()
.sessionCreationPolicy(SessionCreationPolicy.STATELESS)
```

Next, add the two dependencies to *WebSecurityConfig* as we are going to use them shortly.

```
@Autowired
private CommentStoreAuthenticationSuccessHandler
authenticationSuccessHandler;

@Autowired
private RestAuthenticationEntryPoint
restAuthenticationEntryPoint;
```

CommentStoreAuthenticationSuccessHandler will handle success on form-based logins, and the class reimplements the *SavedRequestAware-AuthenticationSuccessHandler*, which is usually used and removes any redirect which is normally used by Spring Security form-based logins.

RestAuthenticationEntryPoint is the same as in the JWT variant and only returns an HTTP 401 on any authentication failures.

Next, we define *CommentStoreAuthenticationSuccessHandler* as a Spring Bean by adding:

```
@Bean
public CommentStoreAuthenticationSuccessHandler
```

```
    mySuccessHandler()
{
    return new CommentStoreAuthenticationSuccessHandler();
}
```

The next step is to configure authentication in the *configure* method like we did in the examples before.

The first thing we do is to enable and configure Cross-Site Request Forgery protection in Spring Security.

```
http.csrf()
        .csrfTokenRepository(
            CookieCsrfTokenRepository
            .withHttpOnlyFalse()
        )
```

Spring Security comes with CSRF protection out of the box. It will generate, by default, a session wide token that must be submitted on each changing requests, i.e., POST, PUT, DELETE. By default, the token is expected to be in the parameters, but we can change it with *csrfTokenRepository* and provide different CSRF-Token handling.

CookieCsrfTokenRepository writes the CSRF-Token to a cookie named *XSRF-TOKEN* and expectes the submitted token in the HTTP header *X-XSRF-TOKEN*. It is following the mechanism and naming that Angular provides out of the box.

When Angular detects the *XSRF-TOKEN* cookie, it will add its value automatically as the *X-XSRF-TOKEN* header for each subsequent request.

Using *withHttpOnlyFalse()* will enable Javascript, our SPA, to read the cookie value.

You can change the name of the tokens with the Spring Security builder syntax in case your SPA follows other conventions.

The CSRF cookie is created on first contact with the application (like the JSESSIONID).

In this example, we are still going to use CORS and keep it as configured in *WebConfig*. However, we need to make Spring Security CORS-aware, so that endpoints generated by Spring Security can run with CORS.

To do so, just add

```
.and()
    .cors()
```

As with the JWT variant, we do want plain HTTP status codes in case of an authentication error and not some HTML. So, as before we add

```
.exceptionHandling()
.authenticationEntryPoint(restAuthenticationEntryPoint)
```

The next step is to reconfigure the *authorizeRequests* part and enable both basic auth and a form based login. However, the login form stays in the SPA, and we only use the endpoint Spring Security provides and disable any server side forms and redirects.

```
.authorizeRequests()
    .antMatchers(HttpMethod.OPTIONS).permitAll()
    .antMatchers("/preauth").permitAll()
    .anyRequest().authenticated()
    .and()
        .httpBasic()
    .and()
        .formLogin()
        .loginProcessingUrl("/authenticate")
            .successHandler(authenticationSuccessHandler)
            .failureHandler(
                new SimpleUrlAuthenticationFailureHandler())
        .and()
        .logout().logoutSuccessHandler(
            new HttpStatusReturningLogoutSuccessHandler()
        );
```

/preauth is a simple endpoint we provide which essentially does nothing but is used for the first contact with the API so that we retrieve the CSRF Token and session id.

formLogin enables form based login, and with *loginProcessingUrl* we change the login URL from */login* to */authenticate* which we are using already in the SPA.

With *successHandler* and *failureHandler* we replace the default behavior of the form based login and remove the redirects and send only HTTP status codes.

logout provides a logout for the application under the default endpoint */logout*.

logoutSuccessHandler also changes the default behavior of redirects to a simple HTTP status code.

Usually, the logout can be done with a simple GET request to */logout*. However, when CSRF protection is enabled, the log out changes to a POST and also requires the CSRF Token to be sent. The latter is done automatically by using *CookieCsrfTokenRepository*, but we need to adjust the log out in the SPA.

We are done on the back end and will change our SPA now.

In *authentication.service* we must change the *login* method to use a form post. But, before we can successfully log in, we must obtain a CSRF Token cookie. For that, we make a simple get call to */preauth* (which does nothing) and receive the token.

While using session based authentication together with CORS, we must explicitly tell the browser that it must send credentials with the request. A cookie counts as a credential. To do so, each request needs a *RequestOptions* configuration with *withCredentials: true*.

The same is valid for the back end and we must allow credentials in CORS by setting *allowCredentials(true)* in *WebConfig*. Only when enabled on both sides are credentials accepted.

```
login(username: string, password: string) {
    const body = new URLSearchParams();
    body.set("username", username);
    body.set("password", password);
```

```
let headers = new Headers();
headers.append('Content-Type',
               'application/x-www-form-urlencoded');

let options = new RequestOptions(
    { headers: headers,
      withCredentials: true
    }
);

return this.http.get(this.server + "/preauth",
                       options
)
.flatMap(
    () => {
        return this.http.post(
                       this.server + "/authenticate",
                       body.toString(),
                       options
        )
        .map(
            (response: Response) => {
                if( response.status === 200) {
                    localStorage.setItem('currentUser',
                      JSON.stringify(
                          { user: username,
                            token: "na"
                          }
                      )
                    );
                }
            });
    }
);
}
```

With *flatMap*, both requests are executed in a row, but only the last one can return the value. If */authenticate* succeeded, we store the user again in localStorage. However, a token is not needed as authentication is done with the JSESSIONID cookie.

In *comment.service* we remove the *authorization* header and just enable *withCredentials* to send the session cookie with each request.

The last thing to do is changing the log out in *authentication.service* to a form post.

```
logout() {
    let headers = new Headers();
    headers.append('Content-Type',
                    'application/x-www-form-urlencoded');
    let options = new RequestOptions (
        { headers: headers,
          withCredentials: true
        }
    );
    return this.http.post(
                        this.server + "/logout",
                        "",
                        options
    )
    .map((response: Response) => {
        localStorage.removeItem('currentUser');
    });
}
```

When you start back and front end now, you can log in and work with the SPA.

Conclusion

Many developers nowadays follow the hype and see stateless API's as the only valid solution. However, by doing so, they often mix up stateful business logic with stateful authentication. Sure, they were often used in conjunction. But you can use them independently and the stateless approach does not make sense for all applications.

However, in regards to security, it is as safe as the other solutions before.

The CSRF attacks, a session based authentication usually is vulnerable to, can be encountered with using a CSRF token flow from cookie to header. In this case, the attacker would need to do the same as in the examples before to get hold of the token. But, different from the previous solutions, it is only one part of the authentication procedure and only valid for a short time.

The bad guy can forge a request to our API but needs to get the value of the CSRF cookie. He could get it with an XSS attack like in all scenarios. However, without it the API denies access.

Additionally, in this scenario the SPA and API run on different domains; we still have CORS as a protection layer.

When your API is a by-product of your application, and you mainly use it to power your application, I think this approach is probably your way to go.

Even when offering a public API it might be worth considering it. Especially, when the business includes scenarios like billing customers for concurrent sessions. Sure, you can implement such things with the stateless variants too, but it is not their purpose.

We did that once in a project. The primary API was stateless with token authentication. However, the business still wanted an alternative stateful API, so they can keep selling an older business package. It was possible but at the price of development and maintenance time.

Recap

Before we continue, let's review what we have covered and check your understanding with a short quiz.

- Remove withCredentials: true in the SPA and examine the request in the browsers dev tool. What happens?

- Is a session based authentication without CSRF secure?

- How do you configure the CSRF Token to be passed as cookie and come back as a header?

Stateful Microservice with SPA Integrated

In the last scenario, we combine the SPA and microservice into one application on the same domain. You can find the source code in the *session_singleapp_csrf* branch.

Overview

In this version, we put the SPA inside of the Spring Boot application, so it is the same app and domain from a Browser's perspective (Figure 4).

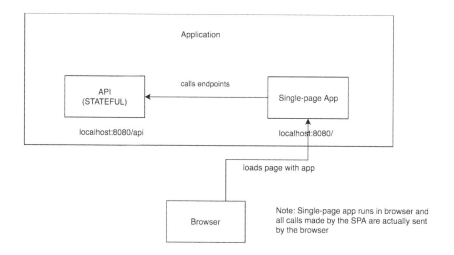

Figure 4: API and SPA Stateful and Integrated

51

In this scenario, CORS does not apply anymore because both are loaded from the same domain. However, as we still use the stateful cookie-based authentication, CSRF protection still applies.

Furthermore, we move the Login screen to the Spring Boot application now, and the SPA does not need to handle it anymore. It will be loaded after a successful login (Figure 4b).

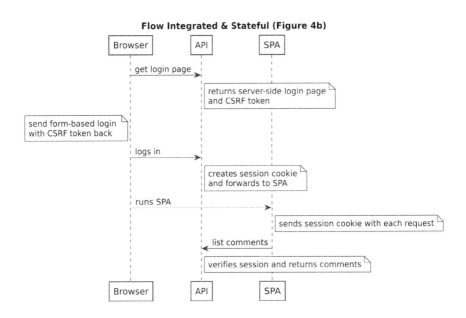

Flow Integrated & Stateful (Figure 4b)

One first request the Spring Boot application detects that the user is not logged in and shows a server-side rendered login form. The user authenticates now, and the application sets a session cookie accordingly and forwards to the main pages, which loads the SPA.

In the SPA, the user is already authenticated and can make requests, which are all authenticated by the session cookie.

Implementation

We will keep the API though and make it available under *api*, and it can still be used with other clients. However, our SPA will be inside the Spring Boot application and completely behind its security layer.

We are starting from the previous stateful authentication version and migrating.

The API gets a prefix so that we can distinguish it from the rest. Add the *@RequestMapping* annotation to *ReadController* and *WriteController* and set the value to *"/api"*.

We are also splitting the *WebSecurityConfig* into two parts. One for the */api* endpoint and one for providing the start page for the SPA.

Like before, we move the *configure* section into its own *Configuration* class named *ApiWebSecurityConfigurationAdapter* and append directly behind *http* a path matcher.

```
.antMatcher("/api/**")
```

The matcher defines which URL path this security configuration is valid for. When you have multiple in place, you need to separate them by paths. As we moved the API to */api*, we include everything under it.

Our API endpoint will work now as before.

Next, we create a *Configuration* for our UI naming it *UIWebSecurity-ConfigurerAdapter* and setting the *@Order* to a different value and giving it a lower priority than the API config. Lower values mean here higher priority.

```
protected void configure(HttpSecurity http) throws
Exception {
    http.csrf()
        .csrfTokenRepository(
            CookieCsrfTokenRepository
            .withHttpOnlyFalse()
        )
    .and()
```

```
        .authorizeRequests()
            .antMatchers("/").authenticated()
        .anyRequest().authenticated()
        .and()
            .formLogin()
                .defaultSuccessUrl("/", true)
        .and()
            .logout()
                .permitAll();
}
```

We will also enable CSRF protection and use the *CookieCsrfTokenRepository* for the cookie to header workflow. On first access to the UI, the CSRF token is created and stored in the cookie. Both, the UI with its login form and the API use the same mechanism.

We will provide a new resource accessible under the root path and require authentication for it. Implementation follows in a few seconds.

We also enable form-based login, but this time we want to use the server side form and let Spring MVC autogenerate one too. The only thing we change is setting a default URL after successful login. So each time we log in, we redirect to the root path as we do have only one single page.

Next, we define the resource working on the root path. For that, we will use the generated index page when building the Angular application.

In the _frontend_folder execute

```
ng build
```

It will create a distributable version of the SPA in the *dist* folder. Copy the *index.html* in it to *backend/src/main/resources/templates*.

Next, we must define that Spring MVC delivers the file when the root path is accessed. As no custom logic is required, we can add a simple mapping in
WebConfig by overriding the *addViewControllers* method.

```
public void addViewControllers(
    ViewControllerRegistry registry
) {
    registry.addViewController("/").setViewName("index");
}
```

However, delivering only the index page is not enough. We must provide the Javascript and other static files too. We will make these accessible on the path */res*.

In the index page above, you need to adjust the script path and append a *res/ in the _src* attributes.

For actual delivery of the files, we use a resource loading mechanism of Spring MVC and map the virtual path */res* to the *dist* folder on your disk.

Create a new *Configuration* class naming *StaticResourceConfiguration* along with the other *Configuration* classes and as it is MVC related, extend from *WebMvcConfigurerAdapter*.

```
@Configuration
public class StaticResourceConfiguration extends
    WebMvcConfigurerAdapter
{

    private static final Logger LOG = LoggerFactory
        .getLogger(StaticResourceConfiguration.class);


    @Value("${static.path}")
    private String staticPath;

    @Override
    public void addResourceHandlers(
        ResourceHandlerRegistry registry
    ) {

        if (staticPath != null) {

            LOG.info("Serving static content from " +
                staticPath);
```

```
        registry.addResourceHandler("/res/**")
                .addResourceLocations(
                        "file:" + staticPath
                );
    }
}
```

The directory is not hard coded but defined by a parameter, and we inject it with

@Value on a field. The actual value is set as a command line parameter when starting the application.

In *addResourceHandlers* we use the *ResourceHandlerRegistry* and add a new mapping telling Spring MVC that every resource that is requested under */res/* is found in the *staticPath* directory.

When starting the application, add the parameter like

```
--static.path=absolute path to your dist directory in
frontend
```

Launch the application now, and you should be able to log in now and see the start page of the SPA again. However, we did not pass the security settings in the SPA yet.

Remove the *canActivate* configuration on the *commentlist* route in *app.routing* to remove the guarding in the SPA.

Now the full application works again.

Conclusion

This version resembles the traditional web applications with a server side UI. Instead of letting the server handle all page generation, we only deliver one - the start page for the SPA. The rest is done in the browser again.

The same constraints apply as with the previous stateful authentication version. Without a CSRF token flow, the application would be vulnerable to CSRF, too. With it in place, no.

The difference is that we could completely use CORS to forbid access to any other browser based application. Our SPA is loaded from the same domain and is not affected by it.

When you come from a single monolith application background and are used to write server-side UI code, it's probably the best way to test the waters of single-page applications.

It's also a good way to migrate server-side UIs step by step to a new single-page application and an API. You can start with picking a component of your application where it makes the most sense. Gaining experience and know-how for future migrations.

When you start out a new application and does not need a public API but don't want to use any server-side UI frameworks, it's a good middle way without losing any flexibility.

Recap

This was the last scenario. Let's review what we have covered and check your understanding with a short quiz.

- Is it more or less secure than the other scenarios?

- Can you use multiple Spring MVC configurations at the same time?

- Is the SPA started before a login attempt?

Conclusion

I know what question is now in your mind.

Which one do I use now?

Right?

It's a tough call, and the only honest answer to it is: It depends.

It depends on a lot of factors.

The type of application you are building.

If you are providing a private or public API?

How many users will use it?

Are any traffic estimates possible?

Does your team have the know-how to build it?

Can your team support it?

And much more.

However, I'll try to shed some light on it.

Each version works in regards to security. If you carefully implemented it and also do your best to prevent XSS attacks you can stop worrying so much. However, keep in mind that nothing is secure and it is just a matter of time until someone can breach it due to bugs, etc.

However, there's no need for panic anymore.

Now with this out of the way, what's left is to choose one based on their pros and cons and evaluate them in your particular context.

As I don't know your use cases, I am going to share some of my thought flows.

I prefer to split the application into an API and one or more UI's (think web and mobile). It doesn't matter if there are any business plans in opening and selling the API now. It's giving you flexibility from the start and forces you from the beginning to separate your back end from the front end. You are obliged to put some thoughts upfront in it before you even write code. It's also a benefit having one common back end handling the business logic that can be used for all of your UIs. New client? Just put it on top of the API.

I've often seen the rise of spaghetti code in service-side UI's because there was no real separation and you ended up with business logic in the UI templates. Always. There was always at least one guy doing it.

However, there is no guarantee it won't happen in an API/SPA combination. The chance of finding these issues earlier are way better. In a traditional server-side UI application, these things can stay undetected for years.

On the contrary, I had the experience that these issues arise pretty fast in API/SPA applications.

The easiest way to start with this way is to use the last version - stateful authentication and SPA/backend in one server side application.

When there are multiple UI's like web, iOS, and Android, in place, I'd split the API and SPA and host them on their own domains. In the case of to much traffic, one can throw more servers on it just for the API.

The fastest and easiest migration would be to version 3, stateful authentication but on different domains.

However, when you need to support the use case of logging in once and staying connected forever, I'd switch to stateless authentication with JWT or a similar token based version. In these scenarios, a session will eventually time out, and the user is logged out. The only way to have no session is to go session less.

I'd prefer it over basic auth because if you lose the token it is not as bad for the user as losing a password would be. People use passwords on more than one account, and your users would go through the hassle of creating new passwords.

I'd also go with version 2 when building public customer-facing API's. It's more complex though, and you need to invest some time to settle on a solution to revoke tokens and authorization changes. Blacklists and token life spans come to mind, but the 'how' depends on your context.

However, I'd also consider it if I had to pass user authentication throughout a bunch of microservices in the backend to prevent dependency creep in them.

If the application provides an API either for pure in-house use or the use with technical users/systems, I would use basic auth. The overhead of tokens might not be worth it.

Of course, this is not complete, and your scenario might fall in between two of the versions explained in the book. An evaluation of your concrete context is inevitable.

Thank You

Thank you for taking time and following along. I hope I could give you a kick start for integrating your microservice with a single-page application.

You can read more about Spring Boot on the resource page (http://codeboje.de/sbb2-resources/) of the book and I encourage you to also connect with me. Honestly, if you have further questions, or just want advice on how to continue now, do not hesitate and reach out. I am glad to help out.

You can either reach me via my blog codeboje.de or directly via the exclusive email address book@codeboje.de.

And if you liked it and it helped you, please lend me a hand and give the book an honest review on Amazon.com.

Happy coding

Jens

www.ingramcontent.com/pod-product-compliance
Lightning Source LLC
Chambersburg PA
CBHW070858070326
40690CB00009B/1897